MORE THAN MEETS THE EYE

AUTISM SPECTRUM DISORDER

WRITTEN BY
Kirsty Holmes

Published in 2025 by KidHaven Publishing, an Imprint of Greenhaven Publishing, LLC
2544 Clinton St., Buffalo, NY 14224

© 2024 BookLife Publishing Ltd.

Written by: Kirsty Holmes
Edited by: Rebecca Phillips-Bartlett
Designed by: Jasmine Pointer

All facts, statistics, web addresses and URLs in this book were verified as valid and accurate at time of writing. No responsibility for any changes to external websites or references can be accepted by either the author or publisher.

Cataloging-in-Publication Data

Names: Holmes, Kirsty.
Title: Autism spectrum disorder / Kirsty Holmes.
Description: Buffalo, NY : KidHaven Publishing, 2025. | Series: More than meets the eye | Includes glossary and index.
Identifiers: ISBN 9781534547612 (pbk.) | ISBN 9781534547629 (library bound) | ISBN 9781534547636 (ebook)
Subjects: LCSH: Autism--Juvenile literature. | Autism in children--Juvenile literature.
Classification: LCC RC553.A88 H656 2025 | DDC 616.85'882--dc23

All rights reserved.
No part of this book may be reproduced in any form without permission in writing from the publisher, except by a reviewer.

Manufactured in the United States of America

CPSIA compliance information: Batch #CSKH25
For further information contact Greenhaven Publishing LLC at 1-844-317-7404.

Please visit our website, www.greenhavenpublishing.com.
For a free color catalog of all our high-quality books, call toll free 1-844-317-7404.

Find us on

ABOUT THIS BOOK

"...right from the start, from the time someone came up with the word 'autism', the condition has been judged from the outside, by its appearances, and not from the inside according to how it is experienced."
(Donna Williams, 1996)

But not this time...

This book was written by an autistic author, for autistic children and their allies.

GLOSSARY WORDS

As you read, you will see some words that look like **this**. The meaning of these words can be found in the glossary on page 31.

CONTENTS

PAGE 4	Key Vocabulary
PAGE 6	The Autism Spectrum
PAGE 8	Sensory Processing
PAGE 10	Self-Care
PAGE 12	Sleep
PAGE 13	Transitions
PAGE 14	Stims
PAGE 16	Autistic Communication
PAGE 20	Special Interests
PAGE 22	Routines
PAGE 24	Masking
PAGE 26	Overwhelm, Shutdown, Meltdown
PAGE 28	Famous People with Autism Spectrum Disorder
PAGE 30	Big Questions
PAGE 31	Glossary
PAGE 32	Index

KEY VOCABULARY

Whether you have autism spectrum disorder (ASD) yourself, you're an <u>ally</u> to the ASD community, or you're here to find out more about ASD, there are important words you will need to know as you read this book.

NEURODIVERGENT AND NEUROTYPICAL

I am autistic. I am neurodivergent.

Neurodivergence and neurotypicality are neurotypes — different types of human brain. Most people in the world (around 80%) are neurotypical. This means their brains are seen as the "typical" human brain.

Around 15% to 20% of the world's population is thought to be neurodivergent. A neurodivergence is a brain difference. Neurodivergent brains work differently than most brains, which are seen as "typical." There are many types of neurodivergence. This means that people with different types of brains will have different strengths and face different challenges.

An example of a neurodivergence is ASD. Another example is ADHD.

I am dyslexic, so I am also neurodivergent.

These other conditions are also recognized as neurodivergences:
- Developmental speech disorders
- Dyslexia
- Dysgraphia
- Dyspraxia
- Dyscalculia
- Dysnomia
- Intellectual <u>disability</u>
- Tourette's syndrome

Neurodiversity is a word that describes all of the different neurotypes together. A group that includes people with different neurotypes is a neurodiverse group. Humanity is neurodiverse.

A person not on the spectrum is allistic. Allistic people can be neurodivergent too, in other ways.

IDENTITY FIRST OR PERSON FIRST?

QUESTION: Should I say "autistic person" or "person with autism"?

EXPLANATION:

Person-First Language: "Person with autism"

This way of describing people with ASD puts their importance as a human first, and their difference or disability second. Many people think this is the more respectful choice, and some people think it is better to separate the person from their disability or difference this way.

But not everyone agrees — and not everyone has to use the same words to describe themselves.

Identity-First Language: "Autistic person"

Many people in the ASD community prefer "autistic person." They prefer to recognize their condition or neurotype as an important part of who they are. Putting "autistic" before "person" reminds you that autism is an important part of who they are and not something they "have" separate from themselves.

ANSWER: If you have ASD, you can choose which language you prefer for yourself. If you are talking to or about an autistic person, it's polite to ask them which they prefer.

THE AUTISM SPECTRUM

WHAT IS ASD?

Autism spectrum disorder is a neurotype. People with ASD are born autistic, and we will remain autistic all our lives. Autism is not an illness. It is a normal, if different, way of being human. Between 1% and 2% of people are thought to be autistic.

All humans have some strengths and some challenges. People with ASD tend to have different strengths and challenges than neurotypical people. These specific strengths and challenges are called autistic traits. While we have many traits in common, no two people with ASD are the same. That means ASD is a spectrum condition. ASD will feel and look different for each person.

Some people think this means the autism spectrum is a line that goes from "less autistic" to "more autistic," like this:

LESS AUTISTIC   MORE AUTISTIC

In fact, the autism spectrum is more like a color wheel. In the picture here, each color on the wheel represents one common trait of ASD. Each person with ASD will experience these traits in different amounts. So, if you plot a person's traits on a wheel instead of a line, each one will look different, but they will all be on the spectrum.

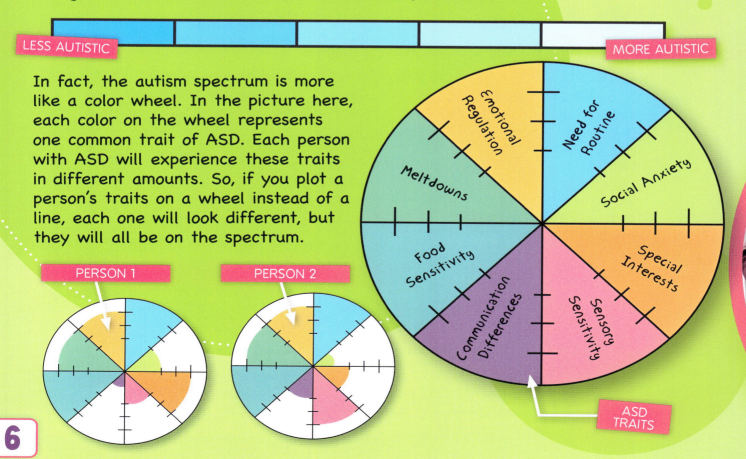

PERSON 1

PERSON 2

ASD TRAITS

A DIFFERENCE OR A DISABILITY?

"Disability" means a condition or difference of the body or mind that makes some activities more difficult or impossible to do. Different disabilities make it harder to do different things.

ASD is a difference, not an illness, but it is also a disability. Since most people are neurotypical, the world is built to work for them. People with ASD have differences in the way we communicate and understand the world around us. This can make it harder for us to live our lives, and we often face extra difficulties that a neurotypical person might not experience.

Some people with ASD use a **service dog**. These dogs are specially trained to help us feel calm, keep space around us in public, and help with other challenges we may face.

This is Aidan. Aidan's teaching assistant, Sam, helps him learn. Aidan needs to learn slowly and quietly. Sam helps Aidan learn things his way.

SAM (ALLISTIC)

AIDAN (AUTISTIC)

SUPPORT NEEDS

Sometimes, people with ASD need help. These are called support needs. Support needs could be a person, a different way of doing things, or a clever piece of technology. Some people need support with the activities of life, including shopping, learning, or working. Some of us only need help outside our homes. Others need help in some situations, such as the supermarket, and not in others, such as a familiar friend's house. Other people need a lot of help all the time. Each person's support needs are different because each disabled person is unique.

7

SENSORY PROCESSING

All humans take in information and understand the world through their senses. The five most well-known senses are:

 Sight   Hearing   Taste    Smell   Touch

It can also be useful to understand three more senses that all humans use:

- Proprioception — knowing where your body is in relation to itself, and where things around you are

- Vestibular sense — balance and the sense of movement

- Interoception — the sense of what is happening inside your own body

People with ASD understand the world using these same senses, but often we experience them differently.

HYPERREACTIVE SENSES

Hyperreactive senses are "turned up" too much. For example, sounds might feel very loud or we might feel very sensitive to light. Sometimes, it means we can sense things others can't, such as high-pitched sounds or faint smells. Other times, it is hard to ignore a hyperreactive sense, such as a scratchy label in a sweater. Hyperreactive senses can feel "too much," and this feels distressing and overwhelming.

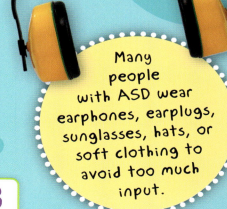

Many people with ASD wear earphones, earplugs, sunglasses, hats, or soft clothing to avoid too much input.

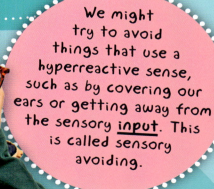

We might try to avoid things that use a hyperreactive sense, such as by covering our ears or getting away from the sensory input. This is called sensory avoiding.

HYPOREACTIVE SENSES

Hyporeactive senses are "turned down" too far. This means it is hard to sense much, or sometimes anything at all, in affected senses. For example, a person with ASD might not sense that they need to pee (hyporeactive interoception), or they might not taste heat in spicy things (hyporeactive taste).

If we are hyposensitive to proprioception, a sensory room can help us feel our body in space. Swinging, balancing, and rolling all help.

This light-up sensory table is covered in sand. Playing in the sand helps if we seek the sense of touch. The soft lights help if we seek visual input.

When we're hyporeactive, it can feel unpleasant. We might try to "feel more" of that sense. If we are hyposensitive to proprioception, we might feel wobbly and **disoriented**, and we might need a hug to get strong input and feel where we are in space. This is called sensory seeking.

SYNESTHESIA

Synesthesia is a rare sensory difference where the senses get "crossed over." A person with synesthesia might hear colors, taste numbers, or see sounds. A common form of synesthesia is "sound-feeling," where sounds can be felt on the skin as though the person were being touched. Two or more senses can cross over at once. Both neurotypical and neurodivergent people can experience synesthesia, but it seems more common among people with ASD.

"Seven is red, and nine is green. I don't know why, but it's always the same. I was surprised to find out not everyone sees colors when they hear numbers!" Saskia, 10

SELF-CARE

EXECUTIVE FUNCTIONS

We all use executive function (EF) skills as we live our day-to-day lives, including while learning, working in a job, or managing our self-care needs such as food, sleep, or housework. Your executive function is like the manager of your brain, helping you plan tasks and remember how to carry them out. We need these skills to listen, organize ourselves, start and finish jobs, and keep track of what we are doing and when.

DO HOMEWORK

EAT BREAKFAST

TAKE A SHOWER

WHAT TIME IS SOCCER?

MATH TEST TOMORROW!!!

Many people with ASD have trouble with EF skills. The managers of our brains might struggle to get the different parts of our brain to do their jobs or work together. Even if we know how to do something, like take a shower or use a schedule, actually being able to put all the skills together and get it done is another matter. This is why we can seem very smart but find supposedly simple tasks difficult.

FOOD

Different foods have different textures, tastes, and smells to cope with, both in the food itself and in restaurants where people eat together. This can cause sensory problems around eating for people with ASD. There are also a lot of **social customs** around food, which we might not understand or remember. And it takes a lot of executive function to plan and make meals. Sometimes, we can even forget to eat if we are really focused on a special interest. Many people with ASD also have gut and tummy problems, which can make eating an **anxious** process — and a painful one. Food can get pretty complicated!

JUICY? BUGS? SOUR? SWEET? DIRTY? SHARP?

Crackers are the same every time. But blueberries can each taste totally different.

Many people with ASD stick to just a few "safe foods" that they know and like. Some foods are so unpredictable or overwhelming to our senses that they actually seem gross, even if the food is fine. This is called an aversion. If we have aversions to foods, we might choose only **bland** or simple foods, and avoid certain smells, tastes, and textures. With patience and gentle encouragement, we can try (and even like!) new foods.

Many people with ASD have routines around food which help us feel safe and in control, such as:

- Eating at the same time or in the same place
- Eating the same foods for each meal
- Keeping foods separate so they don't touch
- Eating foods in a particular order
- Avoiding mealtimes and "grazing" all day instead

SLEEP

Many people with ASD, both children and adults, struggle to sleep. This can be for a few different reasons, such as:

- Struggling to "turn off" our thoughts and settle in bed
- Waking in the night or sleeping restlessly
- Sensory issues (pajamas, bedsheets, toothpaste, noises outside, etc.)
- Hypersomnia — sleeping too much

We can also miss **social cues** at bedtime. These are the signals around us that let us know that it is time for bed — other people around us might dim the lights, put on pajamas, or yawn, but these things might not make us think it is bedtime for us too. If we are thinking about a special interest, we might not be able to stop to sleep.

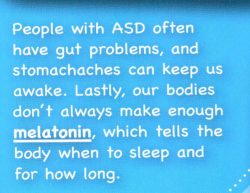

Many kids with ASD use screen time to **regulate** and rest their busy brains at the end of the day, but blue light tells the brain to stay awake.

People with ASD often have gut problems, and stomachaches can keep us awake. Lastly, our bodies don't always make enough **melatonin**, which tells the body when to sleep and for how long.

Good Sleep Hygiene for Autistic Kids:
- Have a simple, low-stress bedtime routine
- Keep your bedroom simple, plain, and dark
- No screens for one hour before bed
- Choose sensory-friendly pajamas, blankets, and sheets
- Create a calm bedtime atmosphere using lights and music
- Use pictures of bedtime routines as a reminder of what to do

TRANSITIONS

Transitions can be:
- Sensory (for example, from being dry to wet)
- Emotional (for example, losing a friend)
- Physical (perhaps going somewhere in the car)
- Social (perhaps starting a new class)
- Mental (switching from one task to another)

For a person with ASD, any transition can be difficult and challenging. People with ASD tend to think very deeply, so moving our focus from one thing to another takes time. If we're rushed into a change, this can be upsetting, even causing a meltdown (see page 27).

Transitions can be small, such as moving from a game to a mealtime. They can also be huge, such as going to a whole new school.

If we are changing from something familiar to something new or unexpected, transitions can be even harder to manage. We might not know how to cope at first and may need extra time to understand and feel safe in a new situation. Routines and schedules help because they keep things predictable, so we can prepare ourselves to make a change. This is why it is very upsetting if our plans change — our plans and routines help us make a chaotic word feel predictable.

Each day can be full of transitions, and each one can present us with lots of new challenges. We just need time, patience, and support.

STIMS

Stimming is short for "self-stimulatory behavior," which means any repetitive behavior a person does to stimulate one of their own senses, in order to cope with, control, or express their feelings. People of all neurotypes stim. Common stims across all neurotypes are:

- Biting nails
- Twirling hair
- Humming
- Chewing gum
- Clicking a pen
- Tapping a foot

Lots of people bite their nails when they feel nervous.

Needing to stim can be especially important for people with ASD. We stim to help cope with our emotions, which can be big and overwhelming. We also stim to regulate hyper- and hyporeactive senses, by stimming one sense to feel in control or block out unpleasant sensory input. These feelings can be big, so the stims needed to regulate them can be big too. Common stims are:

- Finger flicking
- Hand flapping
- Spinning, rocking, jumping
- Pacing or tiptoe walking
- Repeating phrases or songs (echolalia)
- Staring at lights or sparkly things
- Touching surfaces or items
- Pulling hair or rubbing skin
- Stim toys (e.g. pop grids, stretch tubes, or fidget spinners)

Larger equipment, such as a trampoline or swing, is good for full-body stims. Small toys, such as slime or fidget cubes, help with focus and overwhelm.

HAPPY STIMS

Stimming can happen when people with autism experience any big feeling, good or bad. Many of us, for example, flap our hands or fingers when we're happy. When we feel excited, we might need to bounce or spin to help get the big feeling out of our bodies. A big feeling often needs a big stim to help us feel in control of our emotions.

Stim dancing is a great way of expressing big, happy feelings.

ARE STIMS HARMFUL?

Most stims are completely safe, and in fact help to keep us calm and regulated. Some stims feel really nice, and there is no need to stop a person with ASD from stimming. However, there are some stims that are not good for us. Some people stim by banging their heads or biting and scratching their skin. These stims can cause us harm. These stims are usually a response to feeling overwhelmed or to big negative emotions. Stimming like this can be a way for us to let people around us know we are not OK. Learning to find a different stim for that feeling can help us feel better.

Understanding our stims is important — they help us regulate our emotions, keep calm when we are anxious, and feel good in our bodies.

AUTISTIC COMMUNICATION

AUTISTIC COMMUNICATION STYLES

There are many ways of communicating, including making sounds, speaking, writing, using **gestures**, and pictures.

While we're all different, there are some things that many people with ASD share when it comes to how we like to communicate and **interact** with others. These can include:

- Preferring to write or text instead of talking
- Looking away or up while listening in order to think and take in what is being said
- Finding eye contact overwhelming or very uncomfortable
- Preferring meaningful conversation and disliking "small talk"
- Wanting to spend time sharing deep interests
- Speaking plainly and honestly, without "sugarcoating" things
- Needing to be accurate or precise with words, and asking questions to be sure
- Saying exactly what we mean and meaning exactly what we say
- Putting most of our meaning into the words, rather than changing our tone of voice
- Sharing a similar personal experience to show we relate
- Using or practicing scripts to know what to say in some social situations
- Using echolalia — repeating words and phrases from other people or media, such as movies or songs

ALLISTIC COMMUNICATION STYLES

People with ASD generally don't have trouble communicating with each other — but we can face challenges when we need to communicate with allistic people. There are many more allistic people in the world, so this happens all the time. Allistic people have their own communication style too. Allistic people generally:

SID (ASD) AVOIDS EYE CONTACT TO SHOW HE IS LISTENING.

ALEX (ALLISTIC) MAKES LOTS OF EYE CONTACT TO SHOW HE IS LISTENING.

- Show they are listening with lots of eye contact
- Enjoy "small talk" about light subjects
- Have ways of saying things that change the meaning of the words being said
- Use facial expressions and tone of voice to show meaning, sometimes more than their words
- Prioritize manners and feelings above accuracy

THE DOUBLE EMPATHY PROBLEM

When two people with different communication styles interact, they can easily misunderstand each other, especially if they don't know that the other one is using a different style. It is easy to think of direct speech as "rude," or using hidden meanings as "confusing"... But actually, these mean opposite things to each person, and seem perfectly fine to them. If both allistic people and people with ASD learn a little bit about each other's styles, it is much easier to communicate with and understand each other.

I like eye contact...

...but I don't...

... so, I just let them both do their own thing!

JORDAN (NEUROTYPICAL)

REBEKAH (ASD)

CHARLIE (ADHD)

NONSPEAKING PEOPLE WITH ASD

Some people with ASD do not use speech at all, or only speak a few words. This is known as nonspeaking autism. Some kids with ASD are nonspeaking when they are young but later start to speak. A famous example of this is Temple Grandin, who was nonspeaking as a child but later learned to speak. Other people with ASD never speak at all.

Some nonspeaking people with ASD use sign language to communicate. Makaton, American Sign Language (ASL), and British Sign Language (BSL) are all types of signed language.

Just because someone doesn't speak, it doesn't mean they can't understand language they hear or read. Many nonspeaking people with ASD can understand, listen, and communicate; they just need a different way to make themselves heard. There are poets, authors, bloggers, and actors who are nonspeaking.

WHAT IS AAC?

Some nonspeaking people with ASD communicate using Augmentative and Alternative Communication (AAC). AAC can help nonspeaking people communicate using writing, picture languages, or a sign language. AAC can also include devices, such as books, cards, or computers, to help a nonspeaking person express themself.

AAC devices have words and phrases on them, and the user can press a button to make the device speak. This allows nonspeaking people to make their thoughts, feelings, and wishes heard.

SPEAKING PEOPLE WITH ASD

Speaking people with ASD tend to prefer a direct language style, speaking plainly and clearly. We usually mean what we say very literally and are very precise with the words we choose. Sometimes, especially when stressed, we can temporarily find it difficult or impossible to speak. At other times, especially when we like who we are talking to, or when we can talk about a special interest, it can be hard to stop talking! This is called infodumping.

...and horses can run at up to 44 miles an hour and...

We often know lots of interesting facts about our special interests — and we love to share them!

Even for speaking people with ASD, talking can feel difficult or impossible sometimes. This can happen if we're tired or overwhelmed. This can feel like:

- Not being able to remember the right words
- Not being able to get our words out — they feel stuck
- Not being able to make sentences
- Stumbling or stammering over words

Speech therapists can sometimes help us learn to speak, or to speak more if we can only speak a few words. Some of us will never speak, and that's OK.

SPECIAL INTERESTS

WHAT ARE SPECIAL INTERESTS?

Many people with ASD have special interests. These are the things we are deeply passionate about. Often, we spend hours involved in our special interests, learning everything there is to know or collecting everything there is to find. Special interests can be anything, but there are some popular ones, including trains, Pokémon cards, or languages. Special interests can be broad, such as animals or computers, or they can be really specific, focused on a character from a TV show or one particular book.

Special interests often revolve around collecting things and sorting them into groups.

WHAT MAKES AN INTEREST A SPECIAL INTEREST?

Everybody, of all neurotypes, has interests, hobbies, and passions. Special interests, though, go a little further than just a hobby or something you like (although we have those too!). Special interests for people with ASD can be so absorbing that they are all we want to do, talk about, or think about. Special interests can last a whole lifetime or come and go one after the other. Sometimes, special interests can become our life goals, like they did for Greta Thunberg or Chris Packham (see page 28).

Anya's special interest is space. One day, she hopes to turn her passion into a <u>career</u>.

ANYA (ASD)

Special interests bring people with ASD a lot of joy. When we can focus on our special interests, we feel safe and happy. Special interests are often safe, reliable, and predictable things in a world where things can feel messy and unpredictable. Our special interests can also help us feel calm and even sleep and learn better. Sharing our special interests with others is usually a sign we like you!

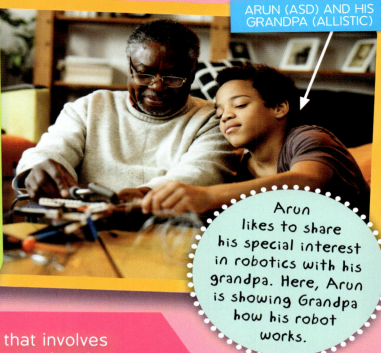

ARUN (ASD) AND HIS GRANDPA (ALLISTIC)

Arun likes to share his special interest in robotics with his grandpa. Here, Arun is showing Grandpa how his robot works.

When we are really into an activity that involves a special interest, we can become very deeply focused. We might forget that we need to eat, drink, or go to the bathroom. We might even get very upset when we have to stop or if we get distracted.

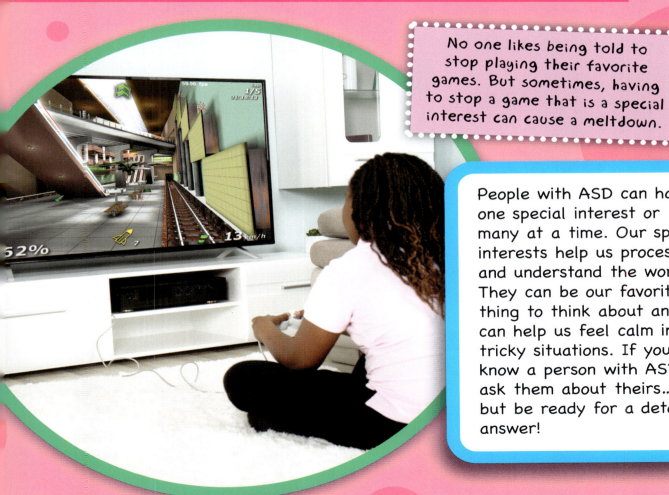

No one likes being told to stop playing their favorite games. But sometimes, having to stop a game that is a special interest can cause a meltdown.

People with ASD can have one special interest or many at a time. Our special interests help us process and understand the world. They can be our favorite thing to think about and can help us feel calm in tricky situations. If you know a person with ASD, ask them about theirs... but be ready for a detailed answer!

ROUTINES

KEEPING THINGS THE SAME

Living in a world that is designed for a different type of brain can be challenging and overwhelming if you don't have the right support. Life can feel confusing, unpredictable, and chaotic. Many people with ASD rely on predictable routines to help us feel safer or more secure. This might mean we need to do some things in the same way every time, in the same order or always at the same time. Making some things predictable and consistent means we have less anxiety.

Aidan and Clara, his **personal aide**, always walk to the library on a Wednesday. They always take the same route, and Aidan always borrows three books.

Examples of some common autistic routines:
- Eating the same thing for breakfast every day
- Always going on vacation to exactly the same place
- Getting dressed in the same order each time
- Having set clothing for each day of the week
- Always sitting in the same place in class
- Always taking exactly the same routes
- Always doing things at the same time every day, for example meals and bedtime

CHANGES

While most people like to have a routine, routines for people with ASD are really essential. The routine feels like the "right" way to do something, and changing the routine feels "wrong." Changes to our routines can be very distressing, especially if they are unexpected. When we feel like things are not as they usually are, we can feel unsafe, anxious, and upset.

Jun always sits in the same place in class. His schedule is on the table in front of him, and his things are where he expects them to be.

MANAGING CHANGES

Changes do happen in life, and everything can't always stay the same. As we grow up, our routines need to change too. Picture stories can help us with planned changes, such as starting a new school or taking a different route. A picture story tells us what will happen, in what order, and shows us pictures of what to expect when we go somewhere or do something new. We just need a little help and a lot of time to feel safe.

WE HAVE A NEW STUDENT

A picture story about a new student in class.

A new student is coming to join our class. They are named Sam.

Our class will change. This could make me feel nervous or excited.

I can say, "Hello, Sam!" and tell Sam my name. Or I can wait to see if Sam talks to me.

MASKING

WHAT IS MASKING?

Sometimes, all people feel like they might need to hide or change things about themselves to "fit in" with a social group better. This can include the way they speak, dress, or the things they do. Humans are very social creatures who usually like to feel as though they are accepted by other people around them. This is especially important in neurotypical society. Fitting in and being seen to be the same as others is so important to us as a species that we do it without thinking about it.

For example, in <u>mainstream schools</u>, students are expected to raise their hand before they speak. This isn't most people's natural <u>instinct</u>, so they need to remember to change their behavior to fit in.

AUTISM AND MASKING

People with ASD are often surrounded by mostly allistic people everywhere we go. Because most people aren't autistic, most things in our society, such as schools, workplaces, and public places, are designed mainly with allistic people in mind. There can be a lot of pressure to fit in to allistic society and appear neurotypical, especially if you are around people who don't know much about ASD. This means that people with ASD can find that they are masking their autism a lot of the time.

Sally feels surprised, so she makes a big facial expression with wide eyes to show Bailey her feelings. Bailey was surprised too, but she wouldn't normally show it this way. But Bailey is masking, so she copies Sally's facial expression to fit in.

SALLY (NEUROTYPICAL)

BAILEY (ASD)

Masking usually means hiding or holding in our natural autistic traits:
- Hiding stims
- Faking a smile, facial expressions, or mannerisms
- Forcing eye contact
- Practicing "scripts" of the "right" things to say
- Talking less or more than we would like to
- Wearing uncomfortable clothing
- Hiding sensory discomfort
- Hiding special interests
- Joining in activities we don't actually want to

People who are masking can look like they are totally fine. But inside, they are working very hard to keep up. It takes a lot of energy to mask.

BURNOUT AND MASKING

Sometimes, masking a little can be useful. Not everyone understands ASD, and sometimes, being able to "pass" as neurotypical can make our lives easier. It can even help keep us safe. But masking all the time is harmful. If people with ASD mask for too long, they can end up unwell and need to rest for a long time. This is called burnout.

UNMASKING

Some people with ASD mask so thoroughly that others are surprised to find out they are autistic. Others can't mask at all. Those of us who can do it have to learn to "unmask." This means noticing when we are masking and allowing ourselves to express our true selves openly. However, usually we need to be alone, around other people with ASD, or with very safe people to be able to unmask.

OVERWHELM, SHUTDOWN, MELTDOWN

OVERWHELM

Overwhelm happens when everything is too much all at once. Lots of sensory input or too many big emotions at once can cause us to feel "overloaded." This can make us feel physically unwell, such as feeling pain, nausea, or dizziness. It can also make us feel as if all our emotions have become very big, and we are feeling them all at once.

During overwhelm, it is difficult to think or to know what you are feeling at all. We can't control overwhelm, and it takes time to calm down.

SHUTDOWNS

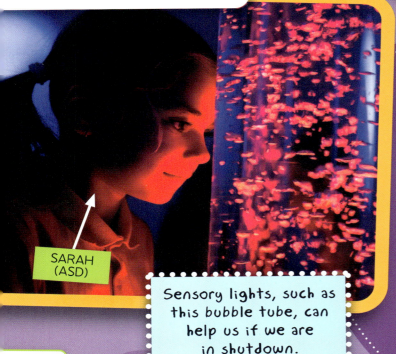

SARAH (ASD)

Sensory lights, such as this bubble tube, can help us if we are in shutdown.

When we are overwhelmed, we can experience shutdowns. In a shutdown, all of our feelings go inwards. We feel very, very tired, and our thoughts can feel slow and heavy. Often, we don't speak. We might try to be still and quiet and block out light. Sometimes, we can stim, for example by rocking gently, moving our eyes, or wiggling hands and feet. Shutdowns can last from a few minutes to over an hour. If we are shut down, others can help us by keeping us safe, helping us rest, and being kind and patient.

26

MELTDOWNS

If shutdowns feel like our thoughts and feelings being shut in, meltdowns are the opposite. All of our emotions become very big, and they need to come out. We might cry, shout, or scream. Sometimes, we might kick out or try to fight with people or break things around us. We might do big stims, such as flapping our hands or bumping hard into a wall. Meltdowns feel very intense, overwhelming, and scary, and can be painful and distressing.

AMELIE (ASD)

Many people think a meltdown is a "temper tantrum," but it is not. We can't control meltdowns, and we don't choose to act this way.

HELPING

You can sometimes spot a meltdown coming — this is called "the rumble stage." We might feel more anxious than usual, stim more, or try to get away from a **stimulus**. Before or during a meltdown, the best way to help is to keep us safe by helping us get to a quiet space, find our fidgets or earphones, and reassure us that we are safe and that you will look after us. We usually just need quiet and calm. Each person will have their favorite ways to regulate again.

FLYNN (ASD)

Flynn's quiet place has low lights and feels small and cozy. He has his favorite music and tablet to help him regulate when he's overwhelmed.

FAMOUS AUTISTIC PEOPLE

GRETA THUNBERG

Greta Thunberg is a Swedish climate **activist**. She became famous for going on **strike** from school to protest that nothing was being done about the climate emergency. Following her regular strikes, soon millions of kids worldwide were striking to protect the climate. Greta says having an ASD diagnosis has been positive for her, helping her understand why she was different from her classmates. People with ASD often have a strong sense of right and wrong. She feels strongly that speaking up for the planet was the right thing to do.

GRETA THUNBERG, CLIMATE ACTIVIST

Greta Thunberg says the climate is her special interest.

CHARLES DARWIN

Famous **naturalist** and geologist Charles Darwin—also on the autism spectrum—actually changed the face of science. Given his neurodiversity, Darwin could hyperfocus on his studies with persistence, and could see details that others simply missed. His neurodiversity was a very great strength, and led to a body of work that is still used today. Difference is amazing!

MATT SAVAGE

MATT SAVAGE, MUSICIAN

Matt Savage is a jazz musician and composer. As a child with ASD, Matt did not like to hear any sounds at all. One day, he taught himself to play a song perfectly on a piano. He was just six years old. Matt is autistic, but just being autistic can't explain this amazing skill. Matt is also a savant — someone born with an exceptional skill in one area, while having a difference or disability in another.

Matt was also able to read at 18 months old.

HOLLY SMALE, AUTHOR

HOLLY SMALE

Holly Smale is the author of the popular *Geek Girl* book series. Holly was diagnosed at age 39, so she grew up not knowing she had ASD. Sometimes people with ASD, especially girls, can mask so completely that their autism can get missed. In Holly's books, the main character is a young girl named Harriet, who is constantly reinventing herself. The books were written before Holly knew she had ASD — but since then, she has said she thinks her character is the same as her.

Holly started making books when she was only four years old!

BIG QUESTIONS

DO I HAVE ASD?

If you didn't think you had ASD before reading this book, but you recognize some of the traits discussed in yourself, you might be wondering whether you have ASD too. If that's you, talk to a trusted adult who can help you find out. If you are struggling or feel like you need help, it's OK to ask for it. You don't have to cope alone, and people can help you feel better about the world.

Recognizing a few traits doesn't mean you have ASD. But if you recognized a lot of things, you might be wondering... do I have ASD too?

Usually, you will start with your family doctor, then a specialist doctor will meet and diagnose you. You will usually do an assessment with your grown-ups, who will talk to the doctor. The doctor will usually ask you some questions and give you some activities to do. This will help them figure out what's going on.

An ASD diagnosis can help you understand yourself better.

Finding out you have ASD can be a surprise, and also a bit of a relief. It feels good to know your true self. Many people find it's helpful to understand their brain and be able to change their life to suit their own unique needs.

If you have ASD, hopefully this book has helped you learn a little more about yourself. ASD research is changing all the time, so there are always new things to learn about our big, beautiful brains!

GLOSSARY

ACTIVIST	a person who tries to make change in the world by doing things such as going to marches
ALLY	a person who is not part of a certain community but supports and stands up for members of that community
ANXIOUS	a feeling of nervousness, worry, and discomfort
BLAND	having very little flavor
CAREER	a job, or set of jobs, that a person has for a long time
DISABILITY	a condition or difference of the body or mind that makes some activities more difficult or impossible to do
DISORIENTED	having lost the sense of direction and feeling unaware of place and space
GESTURES	movements that have a particular meaning
INPUT	something, such as information or a sense, that is taken in by something
INSTINCT	the way someone naturally wants to react to something
INTERACT	to communicate with someone or something else
MAINSTREAM SCHOOLS	schools in the general education system
MELATONIN	a hormone that helps with sleep
NATURALIST	a person who studies and is an expert in nature
PERSONAL AIDE	a person who works to help someone with their daily life and needs
REGULATE	to control
SERVICE DOG	a dog that is trained to help someone with certain support needs
SOCIAL CUES	things that people do to indicate a certain meaning, such as an emotion or that something is about to happen
SOCIAL CUSTOMS	accepted and expected social behaviors and actions
STIMULUS	something that causes a change
STRIKE	a type of protest, when people stop working or going to school to stand up for a certain cause

INDEX

ASSISTANTS 7, 22

DOCTORS 30

EMOTIONS 14–15, 26–27

FEELINGS 9, 14–15, 17–18, 24, 26–27

FIDGETS 14, 27

FOODS 6, 10–11

HOBBIES 20

LANGUAGES 5, 18–20

MELTDOWNS 6, 13, 21, 27

PICTURES 6, 12, 16, 18, 23

SENSES 8–9, 11, 14, 28

SHUTDOWNS 26–27

STIMS 14–15, 25–27

TIMETABLES 23

PHOTO CREDITS

All images are courtesy of Shutterstock.com, unless otherwise specified. With thanks to Getty Images, Thinkstock Photo and iStockphoto.

Cover – passion artist, bakulmie03, Alex and Maria photo. 4–5 – Prostock-studio, Dean Drobot, Gelpi. 6–7 – SeventyFour, Alex and Maria photo. 8–9 – Tomas Knopp, graficriver_icons_logo, RedlineVector, Evgeniy_D, Puckung, Krakenimages.com, Aleksey Mnogosmyslov, Ground Picture, Alina Tanya, paulaphoto. 10–11 – Khosro, Tim UR, Sutthiphong Chandaeng. 12–13 – Sergey Nivens, Krakenimages.com, Miridda. 14–15 – Asier Romero, AB-7272, Ground Picture, Roman Samborskyi, John McLaird. 16–17 – Krakenimages.com, CREATISTA, Roman Samborskyi. 18–19 – fizkes, Olga_Prozorova, Roman Samborskyi, Africa Studio. 20–21 – Joaquin Corbalan P, Pepsco Studio, Eichiku, Milan Ilic Photographer, Andrey_Popov. 22–23 – Alex and Maria photo, Rawpixel.com, Mangkorn Danggura, Elena Pimukova. 24–25 – michaeljung, ViDI Studio. 26–27 – pathdoc, ABO PHOTOGRAPHY, Golubovy, ADDICTIVE STOCK. 28 – (bottom left) Istock.com, Grafissimo. 28–29 – Per Grunditz, Ed Silvester, Greta DiGiorgio, CC BY-SA 4.0 <https://creativecommons.org/licenses/by-sa/4.0>, via Wikimedia Commons, Holly Smale, CC BY-SA 4.0 <https://creativecommons.org/licenses/by-sa/4.0>, via Wikimedia Commons. 30 – Krakenimages.com, Pixel-Shot.